EDITED BY HELEN EXLEY

Published in 2020 by Helen Exley®LONDON in Great Britain.
Illustration by Juliette Clarke © Helen Exley Creative Ltd 2020.
All the words by Stuart & Linda MacFarlane, Pamela Dugdale
and Pam Brown copyright © Helen Exley Creative Ltd 2020.
Design, selection and arrangement © Helen Exley Creative Ltd 2020.
The moral right of the author has been asserted.

ISBN 978-1-78485-188-0

12 11 10 9 8 7 6 5 4 3 2 1

OTHER BOOKS IN THE SERIES

Be Happy! *Be You!* *Be Brave!*
Be Positive! *Be Confident!*

OTHER BOOKS BY HELEN EXLEY

Believe in Yourself   Hope! Dream! Live! 365

Awesome Quotes for Strong Women   Go for it! 365

MIX
Paper from
responsible sources
FSC® C015559
www.fsc.org

Helen Exley®LONDON
16 Chalk Hill, Watford, Herts WD19 4BG, UK
www.helenexley.com

Be a Rebel!

Helen Exley

One of the most powerful lessons
in life is to recognize that no one
can give you power,
and many people don't want you
to have it.
You have to find the courage
to seize it,
own it
and hold on!

SHANNON L. ALDER

To me, power is making things happen without asking for permission.

BEYONCÉ

Don't let people walk all over you.
It's your life. If you want something,
you need to get out there
and grab it by the horns
because no one is going to give you
what you want on a plate.

CECILIA AHERN

I would rather be

Opportunity does not knock, it presents itself when you beat down the door.

KYLE CHANDLER

ebel than a slave.

EMMELINE PANKHURST

All our dreams
can come true
if we have
the courage to
pursue them.

WALT DISNEY

And this I believe: that the free,
exploring mind of the individual human
is the most valuable thing in the world.
And this I would fight for:
the freedom of the mind to take
any direction it wishes, undirected.
And this I must fight against:
any idea, religion, or government
which limits or destroys the individual.
This is what I am
and what I am about.

JOHN STEINBECK

When we least expect it, life sets us
a challenge to test our courage
and willingness to change.
At such a moment, there is no point
in pretending that nothing has happened
or in saying that we are not yet ready.
The challenge will not wait.
Life does not look back.
A week is more than enough time
for us to decide whether or not
to accept our destiny.

PAULO COELHO

The most courageous act is still to think for yourself. Aloud.

COCO CHANEL

Stand for something
or you will fall
for anything.
Today's mighty oak
is yesterday's nut
that held its ground.

ROSA PARKS

Screw up your courage.
There is a risk.
But take it.
Or regret it all your life.

PAM BROWN

The only way to remove obstacles
is to face them head-on, just like
the buffalo stands facing the wind.

GOLDIE HAWN

If you come to a thing with no preconceived notions of what that thing is, the whole world can be your canvas. Just dream it, and you can make it so.

WHOOPI GOLDBERG

If it scares you, it might be a good thing to try.

SETH GODIN

In order to be irreplaceable, one must always be different.

COCO CHANEL

A woman's duty:
To look the whole world in the face
with a go-to-hell look in the eyes;
to have an ideal; to speak and act
in defiance of convention.

AUTHOR UNKNOWN

Two roads diverged
in a wood, and I –
I took the one less
travelled by.
And that has made
all the difference.

ROBERT FROST

There is a need to find and sing
our own song, to stretch our limbs
and shake them in a dance
so wild that nothing can roost there,
that stirs the yearning for solitary voyage.

BARBARA LAZEAR ASCHER

Each skirmish with life increases
our courage and confidence.
Each battle won prepares us
for the bigger fights ahead.

STUART & LINDA MACFARLANE

Experiment, have fun,
change your mind,
change the cut of your hair,
change your ambitions.
What you do now stays with you
for the rest of your life.

PAM BROWN

You change the worl

y being yourself.

YOKO ONO

Normal is not something to aspire to,
it's something to get away from.

JODIE FOSTER

The biggest adventure
you can ever take is to live the life
of your dreams.

OPRAH WINFREY

To me, bravery is
to stand up
for what you believe in.

SOPHIE TURNER

I t's the heart afraid of breaking
that never learns to dance.

XIAOLU GUO

A slave is still a slave if she refuses
to think for herself.

IBO PROVERB

I might have been born in a hovel,
but I determined to travel with the wind
and the stars.

JACQUELINE COCHRAN

...there is an enormous
pay-off in terms of
taking risks,
standing up in the world,
and facing it
with courage.

JUDY CHICAGO

Never get stuck in
a comfortable rut.
The horizon is low
and the going monotonous.
Find the strength to scramble out
– find a wider,
if more risky, world.
The views are better
and the chances more exciting.

PAMELA DUGDALE

Don't think

If somebody says no, find a different way
to get to yes by breaking the rules
or thinking differently, in fact do
whatever it takes.

RICHARD PARKES CORDOCK

imits. USAIN BOLT

Real courage is doing
the right thing when nobody's looking.
Doing the unpopular thing because it's what
you believe, and the heck with everybody.

JUSTIN CRONIN

You don't learn to walk
by following rules.
You learn by doing and
falling over.

SIR RICHARD BRANSON

The challenge is to be yourself in a world that is trying to make you like everyone else.

RENEE LOOKS

You were once wild.
Don't let them tame you!

ISADORA DUNCAN

What is at the summit of courage, I think, is freedom. The freedom that comes with the knowledge that no earthly power can break you; that an unbroken spirit is the only thing you cannot live without; that in the end it is the courage of conviction that moves things, that makes all change possible.

PROFESSOR PAULA GIDDINGS

I am only one,
But still I am one.
I cannot do everything,
But still I can do something;
And because I cannot
do everything
I will not refuse to do
the something that I can do.

EDWARD EVERETT HALE

The only difference
between a rut
and a grave is
their dimensions.

ELLEN GLASGOW

Alas – once it was so simple
to be outrageous. Dye your hair scarlet.
Wear a toga to the supermarket.
Polka down the Mall. Now everyone's
doing it. No one turns a hair.
If you want to get on Facebook
you must really make an effort.
Running naked through a cricket match
doesn't raise an eyebrow.
Painting yourself blue from head to toe
doesn't cause a blink.
Think. Try again. If you really have to.

PAM BROWN

Why be ordinary when you can be extraordinary?

RORY BYRNE

Never be bullied into silence.
Never allow yourself to be made a victim.
Accept your definition of your life.
Define yourself.

HARVEY FIERSTEIN

Don't waste your energy
trying to change opinions...
do your thing,
and don't care if they like it.

TINA FEY

You must never
be fearful about
what you are doing
when it is right.

ROSA PARKS

All the strength you need
to achieve anything is within you.
Don't wait for a light to appear
at the end of the tunnel,
stride down there...
and light the ****** thing yourself.

SARA ANDERSON

If you play it safe in life
you've decided that you don't want
to grow any more.

SHIRLEY HUFSTEDLER

Risk more than others
think is safe.
Care more than others
think is wise.
Dream more than others
think is practical.
Expect more than others think
is possible.

CLAUDE BISSELL

I will dare to do
just what I do.
Be just who I am.
And dance
whenever I want to.

SABRINA WARD HARRISON

The opposite of love is not hate,
it's indifference.
The opposite of art is not ugliness,
it's indifference.
The opposite of faith is not heresy,
it's indifference.
And the opposite of life is not death,
it's indifference.

ELIE WIESEL

Your time is precious, so don't waste it living someone else's life.
Don't be trapped by dogma –
which is living with the results of other people's thinking.
Don't let the noise of others' opinions drown out your own inner voice.
And most important, have the courage to follow your heart and intuition.
They somehow already know what you truly want to become.

STEVE JOBS

Creativity is inventing,
experimenting, growing,
taking risks, breaking rules,
making mistakes,
and having fun.

MARY LOU COOK

Come to the edge, Life said.

They said: We are afraid.

Come to the edge, Life said.

They came. It pushed Them...

And They flew.

GUILLAUME APOLLINAIRE

It is vain to say human beings ought
to be satisfied with tranquillity:
they must have action; and they will
make it if they cannot find it.
Millions are condemned to a stiller
doom than mine, and millions
are in silent revolt against their lot.
Nobody knows how many rebellions
besides political rebellions ferment
in the masses of life which people earth.

CHARLOTTE BRONTË

Everyone has talent.
What is rare is the courage
to follow the talent to the dark place
where it leads.

ERICA JONG

You've got to rattle your cage door.
You've got to let them know
that you're in there,
and that you want out.
Make noise. Cause trouble.

FLORYNCE KENNEDY

Work hard for what you want
because it won't come to you without
a fight. You have to be strong
and courageous and know that you can
do anything you put your mind to.
If somebody puts you down or
criticizes you, just keep on believing
in yourself and turn it into
something positive.

LEAH LABELLE

The best way
to predict
the future
is to invent it.

ALAN KAY

When I'm old
I'm never going to say,
"I didn't do this" or,
"I regret that."
I'm going to say,
"I don't regret a damn thing.
I came,
I went, and
I did it all."

KIM BASINGER

Consider the bear who never roared,
or the eagle who never soared,
or the fern who never opened.
Tap your *Mash-ka-wisen*
[inner strength],
walk through your fear,
and embrace your values.
Be who you are!

BLACKWOLF (ROBERT JONES),
OJIBWE, AND GINA JONES

I have learned over the years
that when one's mind is made up,
this diminishes fear;
knowing what must be done
does away with fear.

ROSA PARKS

You have something worth saying.
Find the words to say it, and speak out.

PAM BROWN

The women who get ahead are those who learn to ignore the warnings they've been give about breaking the rules. If you look at the work history of a gutsy girl, you see that she has made her mark by ignoring "orders" and taking some bold, innovative step that wowed her bosses and left her peers grumbling in exasperation, "I can't believe they let her get away with that" or "I would have done that but I didn't think you were supposed to."

KATE WHITE

Every great dream begins
with a dreamer. Always remember,
you have within you the strength,
the patience, and the passion to reach
for the stars to change the world.

HARRIET TUBMAN

We have to dare
to be ourselves, however frightening
or strange that self may prove to be.

MAY SARTON

You are small.
We all are small.
But time and time again
one small person makes a difference.
To a life.
To a community.
To a country.
Take a first step
with courage and tenacity
and others will follow.
You too can change things.

PAM BROWN

*I want (girls)
to feel that they can
be sassy and full
and weird and geeky
and smart
and independent.*

AMY POEHLER

Don't let the fear of striking out hold you back.

BABE RUTH

I would like to be remembered
as a person who wanted to be free...
so other people would be also free.

ROSA PARKS

I am woman, hear me roar.
In numbers too big to ignore
And I know too much to go back
and pretend
Cause I've heard it all before
And I've been down there on the floor
And no one's ever gonna keep
me down again.

HELEN REDDY & RAY BURTON

Don't be bitter
and mean cos
you don't fit in,
it's a gift.

COURTNEY LOVE

The opposite for courage
is not cowardice,
it is conformity.
Even a dead fish
can go with the flow.

JIM HIGHTOWER

Security is when everything
is settled, when nothing
can happen to you;
security is the denial of life.

GERMAINE GREER

I like it when a flower
or a little tuft of grass
grows through a crack
in the concrete.
It's so *******heroic.

GEORGE CARLIN

To love something with a passion
is most wonderful.
It can take everything you have
and shape it to one purpose.
Out of it has grown all great discoveries,
all stupendous creation.
Its fire transforms
but burns.
Only a few have strength enough
to live within its flame.

PAM BROWN

How can you hesitate?
Risk! Risk anything!
Care no more for the opinion
of others, for those voices.
Do the hardest thing on earth for you.
Act for yourself.
Face the truth.

KATHERINE MANSFIELD

If you ask me what I came
into this life to do, I will tell you:
I came to live out loud.

EMILE ZOLA

What other reason
could there be for
getting up
in the morning except
to set yourself free?

ANN MCMASTER

Yoou never git nothing by bein'
an angel child.
You better change yo ways
and git real wild.
I'm gonna tell you something,
wouldn't tell you no lie.
Wild women are the only kind
that ever git by.
Wild women don't worry,
they don't have no blues.

IDA COX

Acts of bravery don't always
take place on battlefields.
They can take place in your heart,
when you have the courage to honor
your character, your intellect,
your inclinations, and yes, your soul
by listening to its clean, clear voice
of direction instead
of following the muddied messages
of a timid world.

ANNA QUINDLEN

*I want to be strong
and empowered.
I want to shock everybody.*

VANESSA HUDGENS

Courage is saying
"No" when all your friends
are saying "Yes".

STUART & LINDA MACFARLANE

I just decided when someone says you can't do something, do more of it.

FAITH RINGGOLD

The question isn't who is going to let me; it's who is going to stop me.

AYN RAND

Ladies, unite. Let us cherish
our freaks and fanatics,
cultivate our obsessions,
hone our anger to a fine point
and never, never, listen
to anyone who says "be reasonable".

JILL TWEEDIE

Young girls are told...
that they have to be this kind of princess...
If I was going to be a princess,
I'd be a warrior princess.

EMMA WATSON

I have the right of education.
I have the right to play.
I have the right to sing.
I have the right to talk.
I have the right to go to market.
I have the right to speak up.

MALALA YOUSAFZAI

${Y}$ou have to make yourself more
obtrusive than anybody else,
you have to fill all the papers
more than anybody else,
in fact you have to be there
all the time and see
that they do not snow you under.

EMMELINE PANKHURST

Keep your eyes
cast down
in the cart track
and you'll never
spot the turning
that leads to
a wider road.

PAMELA DUGDALE

May you always have
the courage to say no.

PAM BROWN

I was determined to achieve
the total freedom that our
history lessons taught us
we were entitled to,
no matter what the sacrifice.

ROSA PARKS

Let us pick up our books
and our pens.
They are the most
powerful weapons.

MALALA YOUSAFZAI

The reward for conformity
is that everyone likes you but yourself.

RITA MAE BROWN

Do it you

It took me quite a long time to develop
a voice, and now that I have it,
I am not going to be silent.

MADELEINE ALBRIGHT

vay.

PAMELA DUGDALE

If you obey all the rules,
you miss all the fun.

KATHARINE HEPBURN

*When you have a dream,
you've got to grab it and
never let go.*

CAROL BURNETT

The only way of finding
the limits of the possible
is by going beyond them
into the impossible.

ARTHUR C. CLARKE

Be a loud voice not a mumble.

AUTHOR UNKNOWN

Better to live
one year as a tiger,
than a hundred
as a sheep.

MADONNA

Being different isn't a bad thing. It means you're brave enough to be yourself.

LUNA LOVEGOOD

The things that make me different
are the things that make me.

A. A. MILNE

I want to be remembered
as the girl who stood up.

MALALA YOUSAFZAI

I intend to spend my old age
being outrageous.
I hope you will spend your young age
being outrageous too.

STUART & LINDA MACFARLANE

You have to believe
in yourself
when no one else does –
that makes you
a winner right there.

VENUS WILLIAMS

If you believe you're right,
stand up and fight…

ERIN BROCKOVICH

Don't follow fashion.
Be the fashion.

PAMELA DUGDALE

Go out on a limb.
That's where the fruit is!

JIMMY CARTER

Let's stop "tolerating" or "accepting" difference, as if we're so much better for not being different. Instead, let's celebrate difference, because in this world it takes a lot of guts to be different and to act differently.

KATE BORNSTEIN

You have to be willing
to step out of the pack and take risks,
even jump completely out of your element
if that's what it takes.

CAROL BARTZ

When someone tells you
that you are different, smile and
hold your head up and be proud

ANGELINA JOLIE

You have a right
to be exactly who you are.

MICHELLE OBAMA

The rules are whatever
you want them to be.

TINA FEY

And the day came when the risk
to remain tight in a bud was more painful
than the risk it took to blossom.

ANAÏS NIN

When the whole world
is silent,
even one voice
becomes powerful.

MALALA YOUSAFZAI

You have to make more noise
than anybody else.

EMMELINE PANKHURST

You must encounter,
confront, life.
Life loves the liver of it.

MAYA ANGELOU

Do anything, bu

If you don't like the road you're walking,
start paving another one.

DOLLY PARTON

Never let habit lull you into lethargy.
Give yourself a shake.
Change the pattern in the kaleidoscope.
Astound yourself.

PAMELA DUGDALE

t it produce joy.

WALT WHITMAN

I have a lot of things to prove to myself. One is that I can live my life fearlessly.

OPRAH WINFREY

You can waste your lives
drawing lines.
Or you can live your life crossing them.

SHONDA RHIMES

Do not wait to strike till the iron is hot;
but make it hot by striking.

WILLIAM BUTLER YEATS

If you do things well, do them better.
Be daring, be first, be different.

ANITA RODDICK

Every time you come to a crossroads
ask yourself,
"Will I wake up in ten years
and regret not taking this path?"
That is the path to take.

TAMARA CONNIFF

Do not go where the path may lead,
go instead where there is no path
and leave a trail.

RALPH WALDO EMERSON

You have a choice. You can gripe
about what people are doing,
or you can go out and get involved
and work your tail off
and change what they're doing.
I much prefer the second alternative.
You feel better at the end,
win or lose.

PATTY MURRAY

Do you really want to look back
on your life and see how wonderful
it could have been
had you not been afraid to live it?

CAROLINE MYSS

Twenty years from now you
will be more disappointed
by the things that you didn't do
than the ones you did do.
So throw off the bowlines.
Sail away from safe harbor.
Catch the trade winds in your sails.
Explore.
Dream.
Discover.

MARK TWAIN

You can build walls all the way to the sky
and I will find a way to fly above them.
You can try to pin me down with a hundred
thousand arms, but I will find a way to
resist. And there are many of us out there,
more than you think. People who refuse
to stop believing. People who refuse to
come to earth. People who love in a world
without walls. People who love into
hate, into refusal, against hope,
and without fear.

LAUREN OLIVER

To the doubters
and naysayers –
your resistance
made me stronger,
made me
push harder.

MADONNA